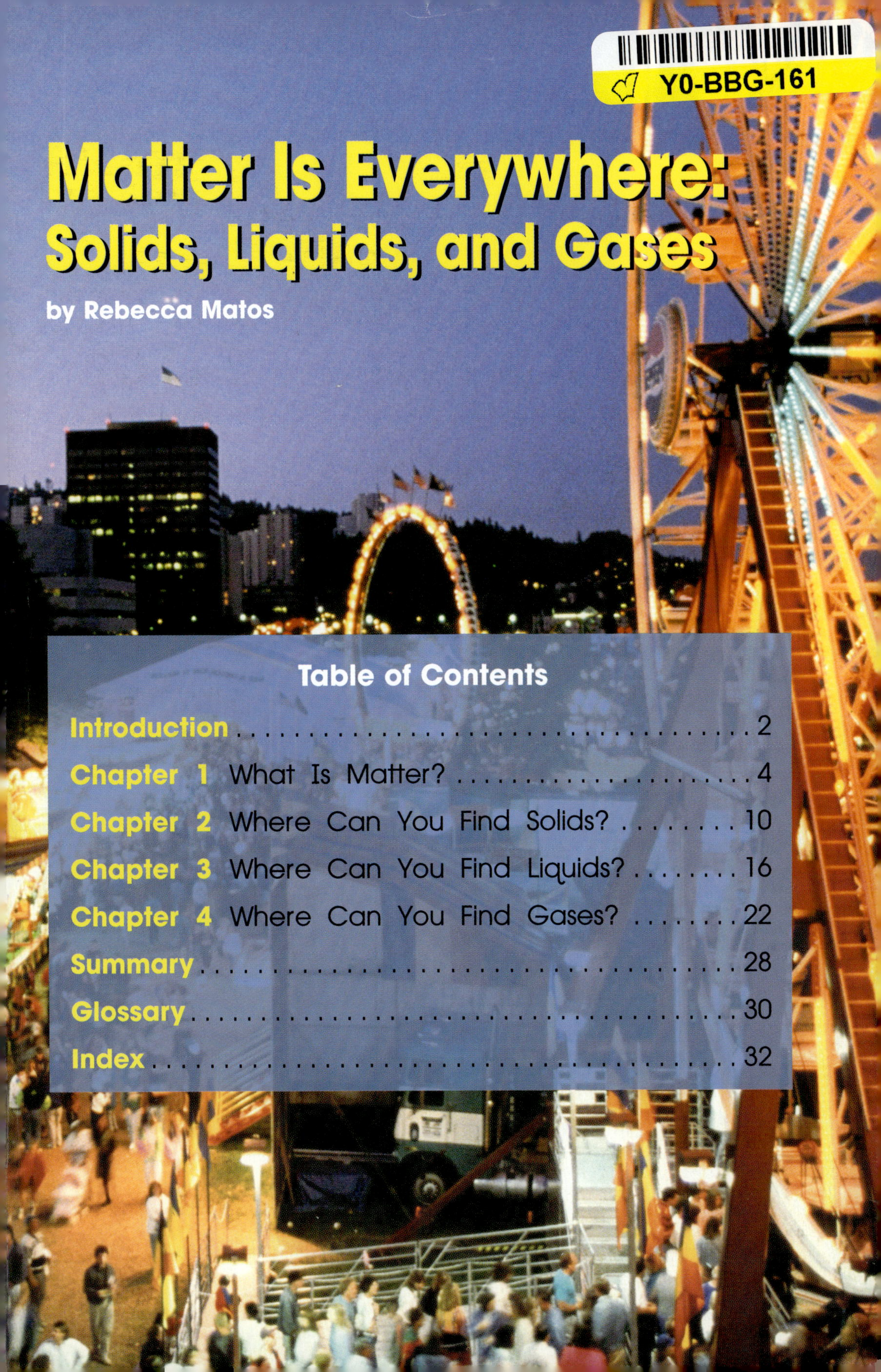

Matter Is Everywhere: Solids, Liquids, and Gases

by Rebecca Matos

Table of Contents

Introduction	2
Chapter 1 What Is Matter?	4
Chapter 2 Where Can You Find Solids?	10
Chapter 3 Where Can You Find Liquids?	16
Chapter 4 Where Can You Find Gases?	22
Summary	28
Glossary	30
Index	32

Introduction

Look around you. What can you see? What can you touch? What can you smell?

Everything you see is **matter**. Everything you touch is matter. Everything you smell is matter. Matter is all around you. Read this book to learn about matter.

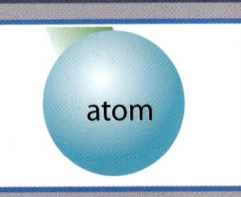

Words to Know

atoms

carbon dioxide

gases

liquids

matter

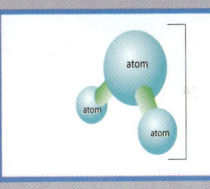

molecules

oxygen

solids

See the Glossary on page 30.

Chapter 1

What Is Matter?

Everything around you is matter. Matter is made of **molecules**. A molecule is a group of **atoms**.

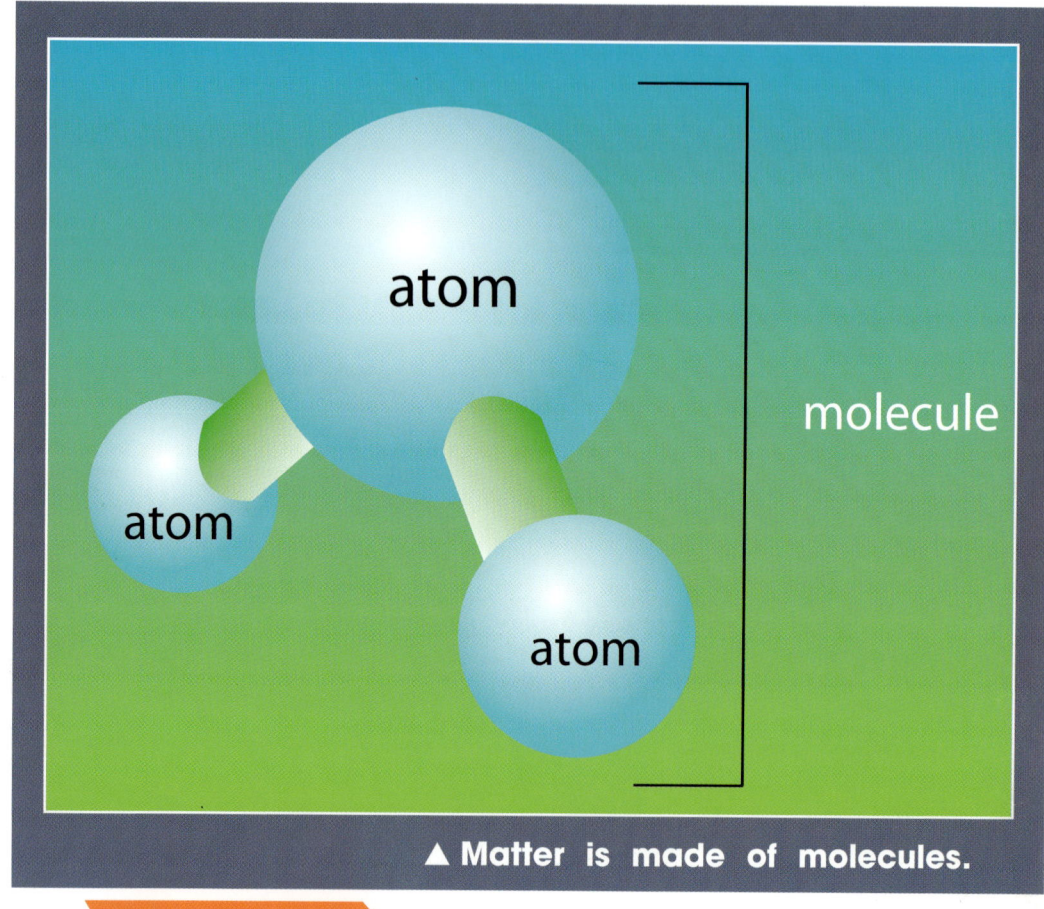

▲ Matter is made of molecules.

Solve This

A water molecule has 1 oxygen atom. A water molecule has 2 hydrogen atoms. How many hydrogen atoms are in 3 water molecules?

Answer: 6 hydrogen atoms

Some molecules have a few atoms. Some molecules have thousands of atoms.

Did You Know?

All molecules are tiny. You need a microscope to see molecules.

Chapter 1

Solids are matter. Solids have their own shape.

▲ A bicycle is a solid.

What Is Matter?

The molecules in solids are close together. The molecules in solids do not move much. Solids do not change their shapes.

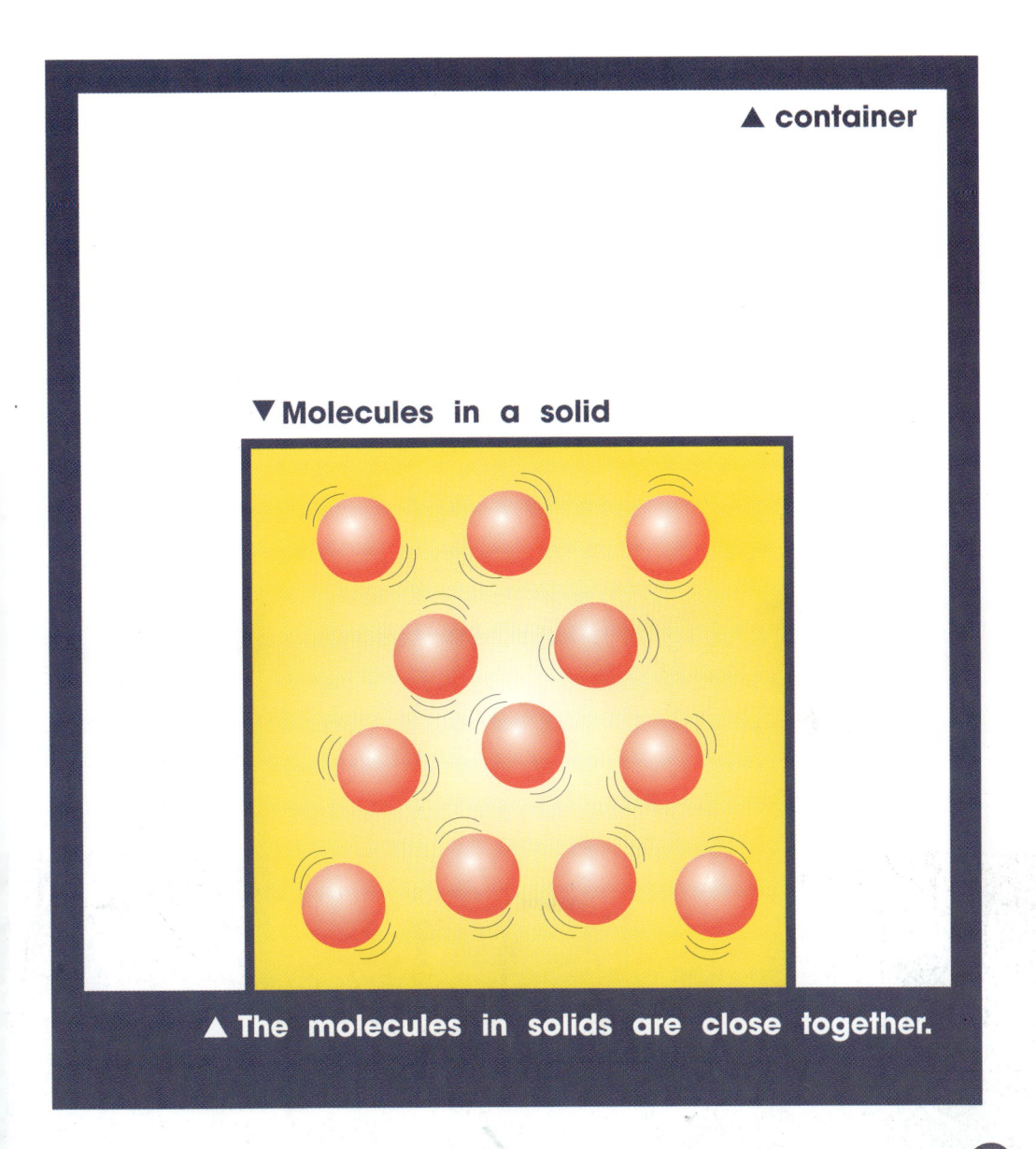

▲ container

▼ Molecules in a solid

▲ The molecules in solids are close together.

Chapter 1

Liquids are matter. Liquids can take different shapes.

The molecules in liquids have space between them. Sometimes molecules in liquids move and flow. Liquids can take different shapes. Liquids take the shape of their containers.

▲ container

▼ Molecules in a liquid

▲ The molecules in liquids can move and flow.

What Is Matter?

Gases are matter. Gases can spread out.

The molecules in gases move. Sometimes the molecules in gases are far apart. Gases spread out. Gases fill the space they are in.

Did You Know?

Sometimes the molecules in gases are close together.

▲ Gases fill the space they are in.

Chapter 2

Where Can You Find Solids?

Look around your classroom. Can you see walls? Can you see tables and chairs?

Walls are solids. Walls do not change their shapes. Tables and chairs are solids. Tables and chairs do not change their shapes.

▲ What solids are in this classroom?

Think about your room at home. What is in your room at home? What solids are in your room at home?

Try This

Look around your room.
1. What solids do you see?
2. Make a list of the solids.

▲ What solids are in this room?

Chapter 2

Now look outside. Do you see trees? Do you see grass or flowers? Trees are solids. Grass and flowers are solids. Earth has many solids.

▲ Trees and grass are solids.

Where Can You Find Solids?

Do you see rocks? Do you see mountains? Earth has many solids.

▲ Rocks and shells are solids.

▲ Mountains are solids.

Chapter 2

Some solids are hard. Wood is a hard solid. Steel is a hard solid, too. You cannot change the shape of hard solids easily.

◢ Wood is a hard solid.

▲ A train is made of steel. Steel is a hard solid.

Where Can You Find Solids?

Some solids are soft. Clay is a soft solid. You can change the shape of soft solids easily.

Did You Know?

Ice cream is a soft solid. Gum is a soft solid. What are other soft solids?

▲ You can change the shape of clay.

15

Chapter 3

Where Can You Find Liquids?

Do you wash your hair with shampoo? Do you drink orange juice? Do you drink milk?

Shampoo is a liquid. Orange juice is a liquid. Milk is a liquid. Liquids are in your home.

▲ What liquids do you use?

Think about your home. What is in your home? What liquids are in your home?

Try This

Look around your classroom.
1. What liquids do you see?
2. Make a list of the liquids.

▲ Liquids are in this kitchen.

Chapter 3

Now look outside. Do you see rain? Do you see a puddle or a pond? Rain is water. Puddles and ponds are water. Water is a liquid.

▲ Water is all around you.

Where Can You Find Liquids?

Water covers most of Earth. Water is a liquid.

▲ The blue areas of Earth are water.

Chapter 3

All liquids can move. All liquids can flow. Some liquids move and flow quickly. Water moves and flows quickly.

▲ The molecules in water flow quickly.

Where Can You Find Liquids?

Some liquids move and flow slowly. Honey moves and flows slowly.

Try This

1. Pour water in a cup.
2. Pour corn syrup in a cup.
3. Pour out the water.
4. Pour out the corn syrup.
5. Which liquid moved quickly?
6. Which liquid moved slowly?

▲ The molecules in honey flow slowly.

Chapter 4

Where Can You Find Gases?

Take a breath. **Oxygen** goes into your lungs. Oxygen is a gas. You need oxygen to live. Oxygen is all around you.

▲ People need oxygen to live.

Now blow out a breath. You blow out **carbon dioxide**. Carbon dioxide is another gas. Trees and plants need carbon dioxide to live. Carbon dioxide is all around you.

▲ Trees need carbon dioxide to live.

Chapter 4

Gases spread out. Gases fill the spaces they are in. The gases have no shape. They have no size.

▲ Gases can spread out.

Where Can You Find Gases?

Sometimes gases fill small spaces. This can is filled with gases. You cannot see the gases.

Try This

1. Blow up a balloon.
2. Put the balloon opening next to your cheek.
3. Let go of the balloon.
4. Feel air on your face.
5. The air is gas.

▲ Gases fill this can.

Chapter 4

Sometimes gas molecules are close together. Many gas molecules fit in a small space.

You can fill many things with gas.

▲ You can fill these things with gas.

Where Can You Find Gases?

You can fill a balloon with gas. You can fill a tire with gas. You can fill a raft with gas.

Figure It Out

Look at the photographs. Where are the gases in these photographs? How are the gases being used?

Summary

Matter is everywhere. Solids are matter. Liquids are matter. Gases are matter.

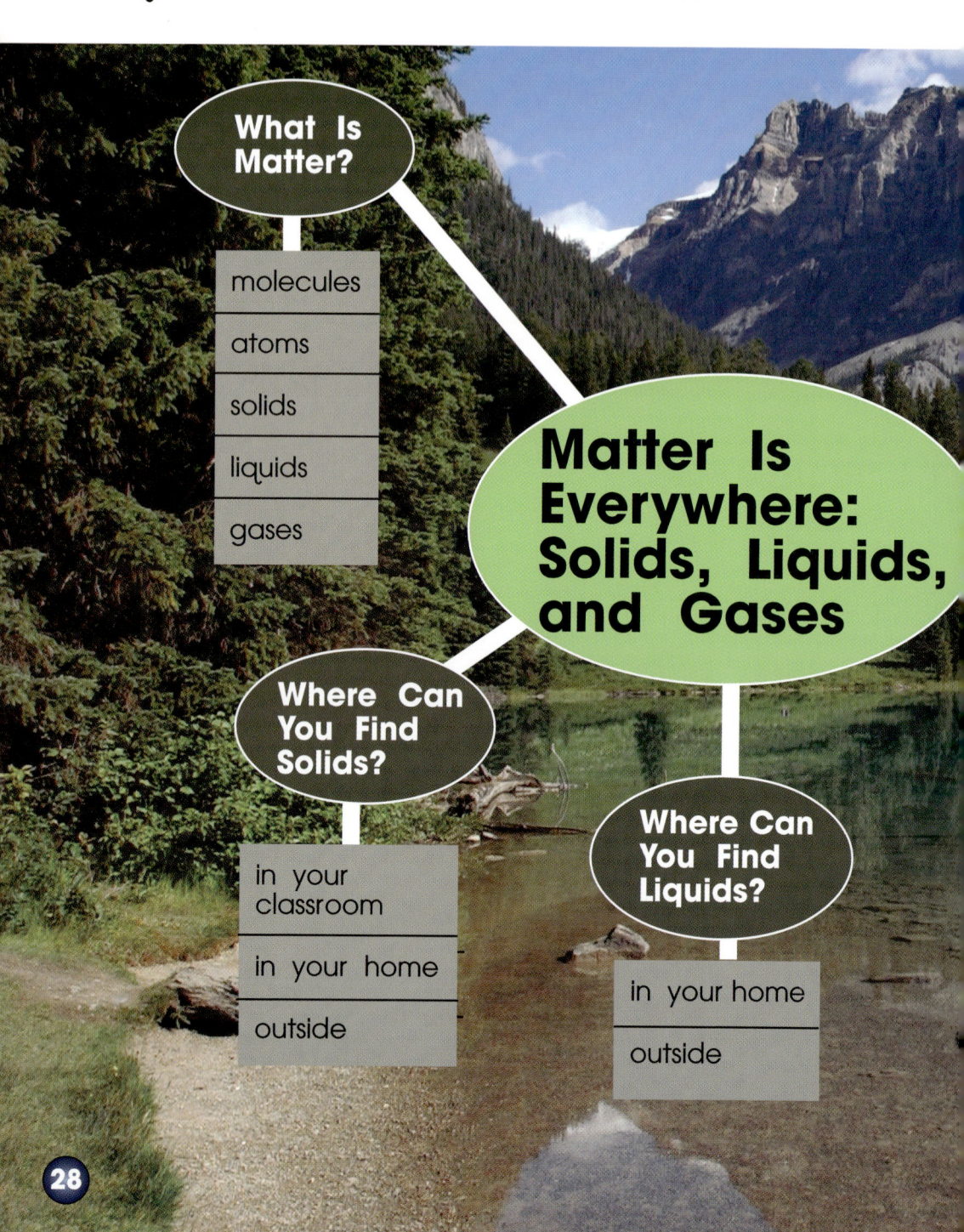

What Is Matter?
- molecules
- atoms
- solids
- liquids
- gases

Matter Is Everywhere: Solids, Liquids, and Gases

Where Can You Find Solids?
- in your classroom
- in your home
- outside

Where Can You Find Liquids?
- in your home
- outside

Where Can You Find Gases?

- in your lungs
- all around you
- in a can
- in a balloon
- in a tire
- in a raft

Think About It

1. What are solids?
2. What solids are in your home?
3. What are liquids?
4. What liquids are in your home?

Glossary

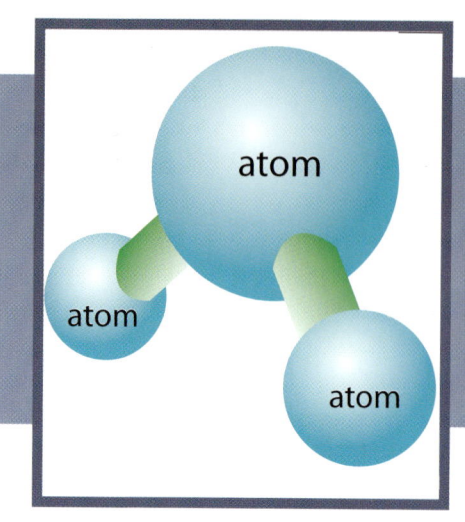

atoms small parts of matter

*Molecules are made of **atoms**.*

carbon dioxide a gas with no color and no smell

*Trees and plants need **carbon dioxide** to live.*

gases forms of matter that can spread

***Gases** are matter.*

liquids forms of matter that can have different shapes

***Liquids** move and flow.*

matter anything that occupies space

*Everything around you is **matter**.*

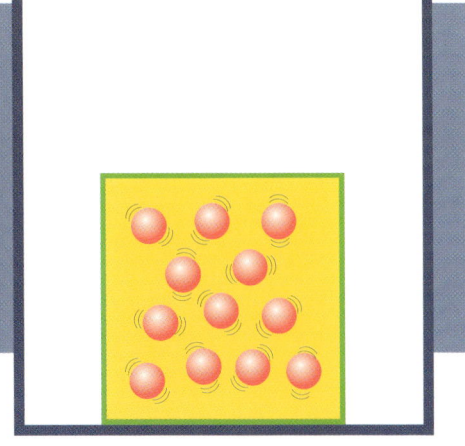

molecules tiny parts of matter

*All **molecules** are tiny.*

oxygen a gas you breathe

*You need **oxygen** to live.*

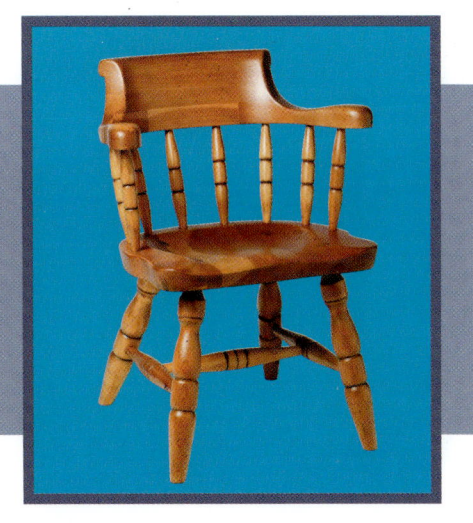

solids forms of matter that have their own shapes

*Wood and steel are hard **solids**.*

Index

atoms, 4–5, 28

carbon dioxide, 23

Earth, 12–13, 19

gases, 9, 22–29

liquids, 8, 16–21, 28–29

matter, 3–4, 6, 8–9, 28

microscope, 5

molecules, 4–5, 7–9, 20–21 26, 28

mountains, 13

oxygen, 22

shape, 6–8, 10, 14–15, 24

solids, 6–7, 10–15, 28–29

space, 8–9, 24–26

water, 4, 18–21